AF440863

* 9 7 9 8 8 6 9 3 5 7 5 3 3 *

UNLOCKING YOUR TRUE POTENTIAL

UNLOCKING YOUR TRUE POTENTIAL

NLP Techniques for over 40 on the Path to Freedom

JOHN BEZERRA

CONTENTS

Thank you to all who supported me:

MOM & DAD
SASHA & LEAH
ANDRE AND STEFF
MIKE
CHRIS
YESENIA ❤

Chapter 1: Introduction to NLP and Mindset Transformation

Understanding NLP and its Benefits for Mindset Transformation

In today's fast-paced and highly demanding world, finding freedom and achieving true potential can seem like an insurmountable challenge. As men and women over 40, we often find ourselves trapped in limiting beliefs and negative thought patterns, preventing us from reaching our goals and living the life we truly desire. However, there is a powerful tool at our disposal that can help us break free from these constraints and unlock our true potential: Neuro-Linguistic Programming (NLP).

NLP is a transformative approach to understanding human behavior and communication. By exploring the relationship between our thoughts, language, and actions, NLP offers practical techniques to reprogram our minds and create positive change in our lives. It provides us with the tools to transform our mindset, empowering us to overcome obstacles, achieve our goals, and live a more fulfilling life.

One of the key benefits of NLP for mindset transformation is its ability to identify and reframe negative thought patterns. Through NLP techniques, we can become aware of self-sabotaging beliefs that hold us back and replace them with empowering ones. By rewiring our thought processes, we can cultivate a positive and growth-oriented mindset, enabling us to approach challenges with confidence and resilience.

NLP also equips us with powerful strategies for setting and achieving goals. By utilizing techniques such as visualization, anchoring, and reframing, we can align our subconscious mind with our conscious desires, increasing our motivation and focus. NLP helps us break down our goals into manageable steps, enabling us to take consistent action and make progress towards our aspirations.

Furthermore, NLP enhances our communication skills, both with ourselves and others. By understanding the impact of language and non-verbal cues, we can improve our relationships, resolve conflicts, and build rapport. NLP teaches us to listen actively, ask empowering questions, and communicate effectively, leading to more harmonious and fulfilling connections in all aspects of our lives.

For men and women over 40 seeking freedom and personal growth, NLP offers a transformative path towards unlocking their true potential. By understanding and applying NLP techniques for mindset transformation, they can break free from self- imposed limitations, achieve their goals, and live a life of fulfillment. This book, "Unlocking Your True Potential: NLP Techniques for Over 40s on the Path to Freedom," is a comprehensive guide that will empower readers with the knowledge and practical tools to embark on their own personal transformation journey. Let NLP be the catalyst for your mindset transformation and unleash the freedom you've been longing for.

Why Mindset Transformation is Essential for Over 40s Seeking Freedom

As we enter our forties, many of us find ourselves yearning for a sense of freedom in our lives. We have spent years working hard, building careers, raising families, and fulfilling responsibilities. However, deep down, we often feel a longing for something more, a desire to break free from the limitations that have held us back and live life on our own terms.

This is where mindset transformation becomes essential for over 40s seeking freedom. Our mindset, or the collection of beliefs, attitudes, and thoughts we hold about ourselves and the world around us, has a profound impact on our ability to create the life we truly desire. And by harnessing the power of Neuro-Linguistic Programming (NLP) techniques, we can unlock our true potential and pave the way to a life of freedom and fulfillment.

NLP offers a set of tools and strategies to reprogram our minds, empowering us to break free from self-imposed limitations, negative thought patterns, and outdated beliefs that have been holding us back. By adopting a growth mindset and embracing the principles of NLP, we can transform our thoughts, emotions, and behaviors, enabling us to overcome challenges and achieve the freedom we have been longing for.

One of the key aspects of mindset transformation is shifting our perspective from one of limitation to one of possibility. As we age, it's common to believe that our options become limited and that it's too late to pursue our dreams. However, NLP teaches us that our thoughts create our reality, and by shifting our mindset, we can create new opportunities and possibilities for ourselves.

Furthermore, mindset transformation allows us to let go of past failures and regrets, enabling us to move forward with confidence and resilience. By reframing our past experiences and learning from them, we can release any self-imposed limitations and embrace a future filled with unlimited potential.

In this book, "Unlocking Your True Potential: NLP Techniques for Over 40s on the Path to Freedom," we will explore various NLP techniques and strategies specifically tailored for over 40 men and women looking for freedom. Through practical exercises, real-life examples, and step-by-step guidance, you will learn how to reprogram your mindset, unleash your true potential, and create a life of freedom, purpose, and fulfillment.

It's time to break free from the shackles of self-doubt, fear, and limitation. Embrace mindset transformation through NLP and unlock the doors to your true potential. The journey to freedom begins now.

Chapter 2: Exploring Limiting Beliefs and Breaking Free

The Power of Reframing: Shifting Perspectives for Freedom

In the journey towards personal growth and self-fulfillment, one of the most powerful tools at our disposal is the ability to reframe our thoughts and perspectives. Reframing is a technique that allows us to change the meaning we assign to situations, events, and even our own thoughts and beliefs. By doing so, we can liberate ourselves from limiting beliefs, negative thought patterns, and self- imposed barriers that hold us back from experiencing true freedom.

For over 40 men and women seeking liberation and a renewed sense of purpose, Neuro-Linguistic Programming (NLP) offers a powerful framework for mindset transformation. NLP techniques provide practical methods to reframe our thoughts and perspectives, empowering us to break free from the constraints of our past and step into a future filled with unlimited possibilities.

To unlock your true potential, it is essential to understand the power of reframing. Our minds have a natural tendency to interpret events and experiences based on our past conditioning. This conditioning often limits our perception and creates a narrow view of the world. By learning how to reframe, we can challenge these limiting beliefs and open ourselves up to new ways of thinking and being.

Reframing allows us to shift our perspective and find alternative meanings for our experiences. For example, a setback can be reframed as an opportunity for growth and learning. A failure can be seen as a stepping stone towards success. By reframing our experiences in a positive light, we can transform our mindset and cultivate a sense of freedom within ourselves.

In the book "Unlocking Your True Potential: NLP Techniques for Over 40s on the Path to Freedom," you will discover the power of reframing and learn practical NLP techniques to implement in your daily life. Through step-by-step exercises and real-life examples, you will gain the tools and insights needed to reframe your thoughts, beliefs, and perceptions.

By mastering the art of reframing, you will be able to break free from limiting patterns of thinking and embrace a mindset of empowerment. You will discover the freedom to choose how you interpret and respond to life's challenges, allowing you to navigate through any situation with resilience and grace.

Join us on this transformative journey and unlock your true potential. Experience the power of reframing and shift your perspectives for a life filled with freedom, fulfillment, and unlimited possibilities.

Identifying Limiting Beliefs Holding You Back

In the pursuit of freedom and personal growth, it is essential to recognize and address the limiting beliefs that hold us back. These beliefs are deeply ingrained in our subconscious mind and often act as barriers, preventing us from realizing our true potential. In this subchapter, we will explore how to identify these limiting beliefs and take the necessary steps to overcome them using NLP techniques.

As adults over the age of 40, we have accumulated a lifetime of experiences, both positive and negative. Over time, these experiences shape our beliefs about ourselves, others, and the world around us. Unfortunately, some of these beliefs may be limiting in nature, hindering our progress and preventing us from achieving the freedom and fulfillment we desire.

The first step in identifying limiting beliefs is to become aware of the thoughts and patterns that consistently hold us back. These thoughts often manifest as self- doubt, fear of failure, or a belief that we are not deserving of success. By paying close attention to our internal dialogue and emotional responses, we can begin to uncover the underlying beliefs that are sabotaging our progress.

Once we have identified these limiting beliefs, NLP techniques can be employed to reframe and transform them. Neuro-Linguistic Programming (NLP) is a powerful tool that focuses on the connection between our thoughts, language, and behavior. By changing the way we think and communicate with ourselves, we can break free from the limitations imposed by these beliefs.

One effective NLP technique for mindset transformation is the use of affirmations. Affirmations are positive statements that counteract and replace negative beliefs. By repeating empowering affirmations daily, we can reprogram our subconscious mind and strengthen new, empowering beliefs that support our freedom and growth.

Another powerful NLP technique is the practice of visualization. By vividly imagining ourselves achieving our goals and living a life of freedom, we can create a powerful mental image that reinforces positive beliefs and motivates us to take action. Visualization helps to rewire our brain and align our thoughts, emotions, and actions towards our desired outcome.

In conclusion, identifying and addressing limiting beliefs is a crucial step in unlocking our true potential and achieving personal freedom. By using NLP techniques such as affirmations and visualization, we can reprogram our subconscious mind and replace limiting beliefs with empowering ones. As over 40 men and women seeking freedom, we have the power to transform our mindset and create the life we truly desire. Let go of the beliefs that no longer serve you and embrace the limitless possibilities that lie ahead.

Overcoming Self-Doubt and Building Self-Confidence

In the pursuit of freedom, self-doubt can be one of the most significant obstacles we face. As men and women over 40, we have already experienced numerous challenges and setbacks throughout our lives. These experiences can often leave us questioning our abilities and doubting our own potential. However, by embracing Neuro-Linguistic Programming (NLP) techniques, we can transform our mindset and unlock our true potential, allowing us to break free from the chains of self-doubt and build unwavering self-confidence.

Self-doubt can manifest in various forms, such as negative self-talk, constant comparison to others, or fear of failure. These thoughts and emotions can hold us back from taking risks, pursuing our passions, and living the life we truly desire.

Fortunately, NLP provides powerful tools to reframe our thoughts, beliefs, and behaviors, enabling us to overcome self-doubt and cultivate self-confidence.

One of the first steps in overcoming self-doubt is to become aware of our inner dialogue. NLP teaches us to observe and challenge our negative self-talk, replacing it with positive affirmations and empowering beliefs. By consciously choosing to focus on our strengths and successes, we can re-program our subconscious mind to embrace self-confidence and banish self-doubt.

Another key aspect of NLP for mindset transformation is reframing our limiting beliefs. Often, our self-doubt stems from past experiences or societal conditioning that has led us to believe we are not capable or worthy. Through NLP techniques, we can identify these limiting beliefs and replace them with empowering ones. By adopting new beliefs that align with our true potential, we can boost our self- confidence and overcome the self-imposed limitations that have held us back for far too long.

Additionally, NLP offers powerful visualization and anchoring techniques that can help us build self-confidence. By visualizing ourselves succeeding in various areas of our lives and anchoring positive emotions to those mental images, we can rewire our brain to associate confidence and success with our desired outcomes. These techniques can be especially valuable when facing challenging situations or stepping out of our comfort zones.

As men and women over 40, we have the wisdom and life experience to recognize the importance of self-confidence in our pursuit of freedom. By embracing NLP techniques for mindset transformation, we can break free from the grips of self- doubt and unlock our true potential. Let this subchapter be the starting point of your journey towards building unshakeable self-confidence and embracing the freedom that awaits you.

Chapter 3: Rewiring Your Mind for Success

Neuroplasticity and its Role in Mindset Transformation

In the quest for personal growth and a sense of freedom, individuals over the age of 40 often find themselves seeking effective techniques to transform their mindset. One powerful tool that can aid in this process is neuroplasticity. This subchapter will explore the concept of neuroplasticity and its significant role in mindset transformation, particularly for those interested in NLP techniques.

Neuroplasticity refers to the brain's remarkable ability to reorganize itself by forming new neural connections throughout life. Contrary to the previous belief that the brain's structure is fixed after a certain age, neuroplasticity reveals that our brains are malleable and capable of change. This discovery offers immense hope for individuals looking to break free from limiting beliefs and patterns of thinking that have hindered their personal growth.

For those on the path to freedom, understanding neuroplasticity can be a game- changer. By harnessing the brain's plasticity, individuals can consciously reshape their mindset and create new neural pathways that support their desired transformation. NLP techniques provide a framework for utilizing neuroplasticity effectively.

Through NLP, individuals can identify and reframe limiting beliefs, replace negative thought patterns with positive ones, and cultivate a growth mindset. By consistently practicing NLP techniques, individuals can gradually rewire their brains to think and perceive the world in a more empowering way. This process enables them to break free from self-imposed limitations and embrace a mindset that fosters personal freedom.

Moreover, neuroplasticity offers hope for those who may have previously believed that change was impossible due to their age. It highlights that it is never too late to embark on a journey of mindset transformation. The brain's plasticity remains present throughout adulthood, allowing individuals over 40 to tap into their true potential and experience profound personal growth.

In conclusion, neuroplasticity plays a vital role in mindset transformation, especially for individuals over 40 seeking freedom. By understanding and utilizing the brain's ability to rewire itself, individuals can break free from limiting beliefs and patterns of thinking that have hindered their personal growth. NLP techniques provide a powerful framework for leveraging neuroplasticity and creating lasting mindset shifts. With neuroplasticity as a guiding principle, individuals can embark on a transformative journey, unlocking their true potential and experiencing newfound freedom in their lives.

Utilizing Anchoring Techniques to Unlock True Potential

In our journey towards personal growth and fulfillment, one of the most powerful tools we can utilize is Neuro-Linguistic Programming (NLP). NLP is a transformative approach that enables us to reprogram our minds and enhance our mindset, ultimately unlocking our true potential. For men and women over the age of 40 who are seeking freedom and a new lease on life, NLP offers a unique opportunity for mindset transformation.

Anchoring is a fundamental technique within NLP that allows us to create powerful associations between our thoughts, emotions, and actions. By understanding and utilizing anchoring techniques, we can harness our innate abilities and unlock our true potential.

Anchoring involves creating an anchor, which can be a physical or mental trigger, that links a desired state or emotion to a specific stimulus. For example, imagine a time when you felt confident, powerful, and unstoppable. By associating this empowering state with a specific gesture, such as touching your thumb and index finger together, you can create an anchor that can be activated whenever you need to access that state of confidence and power.

By consistently using anchoring techniques, we can rewire our minds to automatically access empowering states when faced with challenges or obstacles. This allows us to tap into our true potential and perform at our best, even in high-pressure situations.

To utilize anchoring techniques effectively, it is crucial to understand the underlying principles and practice them consistently. This subchapter will provide you with step-by-step instructions on how to create and activate anchors, as well as tips on how to integrate them into your daily life. You will also learn how to anchor positive emotions and states to specific goals, enabling you to stay motivated and focused on your path to freedom.

Unlocking your true potential is not an overnight process; it requires dedication, practice, and a willingness to explore the depths of your mind. NLP, specifically anchoring techniques, offers a roadmap to transform your mindset and unleash your true potential. By utilizing these techniques, you can break free from limiting beliefs, overcome obstacles, and step into a life of freedom, fulfillment, and joy.

Are you ready to unlock your true potential? Dive into the world of anchoring techniques and embark on a transformative journey towards a life of freedom and fulfillment.

The Power of Visualization and Affirmations

In our journey to unlock our true potential, one of the most powerful tools we can harness is the practice of visualization and affirmations. These techniques, rooted in the principles of Neuro-Linguistic Programming (NLP), have the ability to transform our mindset and pave the way to freedom.

For over 40 men and women seeking liberation from the shackles of self-doubt and limited beliefs, NLP offers a pathway to rediscovering their true potential.

Visualization, the process of creating vivid mental images of our desired outcomes, allows us to tap into the power of our subconscious mind. By visualizing our goals with clarity and emotion, we activate the reticular activating system in our brain, which then starts seeking out opportunities and resources that align with our visions.

Imagine the freedom of envisioning yourself living the life you've always dreamed of. Picture the joy, the fulfillment, and the sense of purpose that accompanies this new reality. Visualization allows us to tap into this potential and create a blueprint for our future. By consistently visualizing our goals, we can reprogram our subconscious mind to align with our desires, thereby paving the way for our dreams to manifest.

Affirmations, on the other hand, are positive statements that we repeat to ourselves regularly. These statements are designed to counteract any negative self-talk or limiting beliefs that may be holding us back. For over 40 men and women seeking freedom, affirmations serve as a powerful tool to rewire their mindset and build empowering beliefs.

By repeating affirmations such as "I am worthy of success and happiness" or "I have the power to create the life I desire," we begin to reprogram our subconscious mind. These affirmations act as powerful messages that override any doubts or fears that may have been ingrained in us over the years. As we consistently affirm our worthiness and abilities, our mindset begins to shift, and we open ourselves up to new opportunities and possibilities.

In the pursuit of freedom, visualization and affirmations are invaluable tools that can help us overcome self-imposed limitations and unlock our true potential. By harnessing the power of our mind and aligning it with our desires, we can create a life of abundance, fulfillment, and joy. So, let us embrace the power of visualization and affirmations, and embark on a transformative journey towards freedom.

Chapter 4: Mastering Emotional Intelligence

Understanding Emotions and How They Influence Your Behavior

Emotions play a significant role in our lives, shaping our thoughts, actions, and overall behavior. As we embark on the path to freedom, it is crucial for individuals over 40 to comprehend the profound impact emotions have on our mindset and transformation journey. In this subchapter, we will delve into the depths of understanding emotions and how they can influence our behavior, using Neuro- Linguistic Programming (NLP) techniques specifically tailored for the over 40 audience seeking freedom.

Emotions are powerful and intricate forces that can either propel us forward or hold us back. By learning how to harness and control our emotions, we can unlock our true potential and experience genuine freedom. NLP provides us with the tools and techniques to identify, understand, and manage our emotions effectively.

To begin, it is essential to grasp the connection between emotions and behavior. Our emotions serve as a guiding compass, steering our thoughts and actions in a particular direction. They can drive us to take risks, make decisions, or even hinder us from pursuing our goals. By comprehending this relationship, we can start to gain control over our behavior and make conscious choices aligned with our desired outcomes.

In this subchapter, we will explore various NLP techniques that enable us to understand and regulate our emotions. One such technique is anchoring, which involves associating a specific emotion with a physical or mental trigger. By creating positive anchors, we can access empowering emotions whenever needed, helping us overcome challenges and maintain a positive mindset on our path to freedom.

Additionally, we will delve into reframing, a powerful NLP technique that allows us to reinterpret and change the meaning of our emotions. By reframing negative emotions into more positive and productive perspectives, we can transform our behavior and responses to challenging situations.

Understanding emotions also involves acknowledging the impact of past experiences and limiting beliefs on our emotional responses. NLP provides effective strategies for uncovering and releasing negative emotions and limiting beliefs that may be holding us back. By doing so, we can break free from the chains of the past and truly embrace our journey towards freedom.

In conclusion, emotions are a fundamental aspect of our behavior and mindset. By understanding and managing our emotions through NLP techniques, we can unlock our true potential and experience genuine freedom. This subchapter has provided an overview of the profound influence emotions have on our behavior, and how NLP can be applied to transform our mindset and facilitate lasting change. As we continue our exploration of NLP techniques for over 40s on the path to freedom, let us embrace the power of emotions and use them as catalysts for growth and transformation.

Developing Emotional Resilience for Freedom and Fulfillment

Emotional resilience is a crucial skill that can transform your mindset and pave the way to freedom and fulfillment. As we journey through life, we encounter various challenges and setbacks that can easily knock us off balance. However, by developing emotional resilience, we can navigate these obstacles with grace and emerge stronger than ever before.

For over 40 men and women looking for freedom, emotional resilience becomes even more essential. This stage of life often brings significant changes, such as career transitions, empty nests, or the pursuit of new passions. NLP techniques can empower you to embrace these changes, overcome limiting beliefs, and unlock your true potential.

One of the fundamental aspects of developing emotional resilience is understanding and managing your emotions. It is essential to acknowledge that emotions are a natural part of being human. With NLP techniques, you can learn to recognize your emotions, understand their underlying causes, and respond to them in a healthy and constructive manner.

Furthermore, reframing negative experiences can help you build emotional resilience. By shifting your perspective and finding the silver lining in challenging situations, you can transform setbacks into valuable lessons and opportunities for growth. NLP provides powerful tools to reframe your thoughts and beliefs, enabling you to view obstacles as stepping stones towards freedom and fulfillment.

Cultivating self-compassion is another crucial aspect of emotional resilience. Over 40, many individuals tend to be harsh critics of themselves, focusing on past mistakes or unfulfilled expectations. NLP techniques can guide you towards self- acceptance and self-love, allowing you to let go of self-judgment and embrace your true potential.

Practicing mindfulness and stress management techniques can also contribute to emotional resilience. By staying present in the moment and managing stress effectively, you can maintain a clear and focused mindset. NLP offers various techniques, such as anchoring or visualization, that can help you achieve a state of calm and balance, even in the face of adversity.

Ultimately, developing emotional resilience is an ongoing process that requires commitment and practice. By incorporating NLP techniques into your daily life, you can cultivate the necessary skills to navigate life's challenges with confidence and grace. Unlocking your true potential becomes not just a distant dream but a tangible reality, leading to freedom and fulfillment in all aspects of your life.

Managing Stress and Overcoming Negative Emotions

In our fast-paced modern world, stress and negative emotions can often feel overwhelming, particularly for individuals over the age of 40 who are seeking freedom and personal growth. However, with the right mindset and the power of Neuro-Linguistic Programming (NLP) techniques, it is possible to effectively manage stress and overcome negative emotions, unlocking your true potential and finding the freedom you desire.

Stress is a common experience that can be triggered by various factors such as work pressure, financial challenges, relationship issues, and health concerns. When left unmanaged, stress can have detrimental effects on both our physical and mental well-being. NLP offers a range of powerful tools and strategies to help you identify the root causes of stress and develop effective coping mechanisms.

One of the key principles of NLP is understanding the connection between our thoughts, emotions, and behaviors. By learning to recognize and challenge negative thought patterns, we can gain control over our emotions and reduce stress levels. Techniques such as reframing, visualization, and anchoring can be powerful tools in managing stress and promoting a more positive mindset.

Additionally, NLP offers strategies for overcoming negative emotions such as fear, anger, and sadness. By understanding the underlying beliefs and values that drive these emotions, we can reprogram our minds to respond in a more constructive and empowering way. Through techniques like timeline therapy and parts integration, NLP enables us to release negative emotions and replace them with more positive and empowering states.

It is important to note that managing stress and overcoming negative emotions is an ongoing process that requires commitment and practice. By incorporating NLP techniques into your daily routine, you can gradually transform your mindset and experience greater freedom and fulfillment.

In "Unlocking Your True Potential: NLP Techniques for Over 40s on the Path to Freedom," you will discover a wealth of NLP tools and strategies specifically tailored to mindset transformation for individuals over 40. This subchapter will guide you through practical exercises and step-by-step techniques to manage stress and overcome negative emotions, empowering

you to unlock your true potential and find the freedom
you seek.

Remember, it is never too late to embark on a journey
of personal growth and transformation. By harnessing the
power of NLP, you can effectively manage stress, overcome
negative emotions, and experience a greater sense of freedom
and fulfillment in your life.

CHAPTER 5

Chapter 5: Enhancing Communication Skills for Personal and Professional Growth

Effective Listening: The Key to Building Strong Relationships

In today's fast-paced world, where distractions are abundant, it is becoming increasingly difficult to truly connect with others. As we age and seek freedom in our lives, it is essential to develop the skill of effective listening, as it is the key to building strong and meaningful relationships. This subchapter will explore the power of effective listening and how it can transform your mindset and bring you the freedom you desire.

Listening is not merely hearing someone's words; it is about understanding their thoughts, emotions, and perspectives.

For over 40 men and women on the path to freedom, mastering the art of effective listening is crucial in nurturing relationships with partners, family, friends, and colleagues. By actively listening to others, we demonstrate respect, empathy, and validation, which in turn strengthens the bond between individuals.

In the realm of NLP (Neuro-Linguistic Programming), effective listening plays a pivotal role in mindset transformation. By truly understanding someone's words, we can gain insights into their belief systems, values, and desires. This deep understanding allows us to identify and challenge our own limiting beliefs, paving the way for personal growth and transformation.

Moreover, effective listening is not limited to verbal communication; it also involves paying attention to non-verbal cues such as body language, facial expressions, and tone of voice. By observing these cues, we can gain a deeper understanding of someone's emotions and thoughts, enabling us to respond more effectively and connect on a deeper level.

To become an effective listener, it is crucial to cultivate self-awareness and be present in the moment. This subchapter will explore practical techniques and exercises to enhance your listening skills, including active listening, reflective listening, and empathic listening. Through these techniques, you will learn to suspend judgment, ask relevant questions, and provide meaningful feedback, fostering an environment of trust and openness.

By mastering the art of effective listening, you will experience a profound shift in your relationships and overall well-being. The ability to truly understand and connect with others will bring you the freedom you seek, allowing you to build strong, fulfilling relationships based on empathy, trust, and mutual respect.

In conclusion, effective listening is a vital skill for over 40 men and women on the path to freedom. By actively listening and understanding others, we can transform our mindset, challenge limiting beliefs, and create meaningful connections. This subchapter will equip you with the tools and techniques necessary to unlock your true potential and build strong, lasting relationships that bring you the freedom and fulfillment you desire.

Non-Verbal Communication and Body Language Mastery

In the journey towards unlocking your true potential, understanding the power of non-verbal communication and mastering body language can be a game-changer. As men and women over 40, we often find ourselves in situations where effective communication becomes crucial. Whether it's in our personal relationships, professional endeavors, or simply interacting with others, being able to convey our thoughts, emotions, and intentions without uttering a single word can significantly impact our success and overall sense of freedom.

Non-verbal communication encompasses a wide range of cues, including facial expressions, gestures, posture, and even the tone of our voice. Understanding the nuances of these cues can help us build stronger connections, influence others, and project confidence. It is a powerful tool that, when honed, can transform our mindset and bring about positive change in our lives.

This subchapter delves into the secrets of non-verbal communication and body language mastery. We will explore how to decipher the unspoken language of others and leverage it to our advantage. By becoming aware of the messages we unconsciously send through our body language, we gain the ability to align our actions with our desired outcomes.

Through the principles of Neuro-Linguistic Programming (NLP), we will learn techniques to improve our non-verbal communication skills. NLP provides a framework for understanding the intricate connection between our thoughts, language, and behavior, allowing us to make intentional changes that align with our goals.

Unlocking the power of non-verbal communication goes beyond mere observation. It requires practice, self-awareness, and a willingness to step outside our comfort zones. This subchapter will provide practical exercises and strategies to enhance our non-verbal communication skills, empowering us to navigate diverse social situations with ease and grace.

By mastering non-verbal communication and body language, we gain the ability to express ourselves more authentically, connect with others on a deeper level, and influence our environment positively. It is a transformative skillset that transcends age and gender, allowing us to break free from limitations and unlock our true potential.

Join us on this journey of self-discovery and empowerment as we delve into the world of non-verbal communication and body language mastery. Together, let us embrace the power of NLP to transform our mindset and liberate ourselves from the constraints that have held us back. It is time to unleash our true potential and embrace the freedom that awaits us.

The Art of Persuasion and Influence in Achieving Freedom

In our journey towards freedom, one of the most powerful tools at our disposal is the art of persuasion and influence. By mastering the techniques of NLP (Neuro-Linguistic Programming), we can transform our mindset and unleash our true potential. This subchapter delves into the art of persuasion and influence, guiding over 40 men and women on the path to freedom.

Persuasion and influence are not just skills to be used in sales or negotiation; they are essential in all aspects of life. Whether we want to convince ourselves to break free from limiting beliefs or influence others to support our quest for freedom, understanding the principles behind effective persuasion is crucial.

NLP techniques offer a unique approach to persuasion and influence. By tapping into the power of language, body language, and subconscious communication, we can create a profound impact on ourselves and those around us. These techniques help us break through barriers, overcome resistance, and align our thoughts and actions towards achieving true freedom.

One important aspect of persuasion is understanding the mind-body connection. We explore the ways in which our thoughts and beliefs shape our reality and how we can reprogram our subconscious mind to support our goals. Through NLP techniques, we learn to identify and replace limiting beliefs with empowering ones, allowing us to break free from the chains that hold us back.

Furthermore, we delve into the power of language and communication. We explore how to use persuasive language patterns, such as storytelling and metaphors, to connect with others on a deeper level. By understanding the power of words, we can influence others to support our journey towards freedom and inspire them to embark on their own path of self-discovery.

In addition, non-verbal communication plays a significant role in persuasion and influence. We explore the art of body language and how to use it to create rapport, build trust, and convey our message effectively. By mastering these techniques, we can establish strong connections with others and influence them towards a shared vision of freedom.

Unlocking Your True Potential: NLP Techniques for Over 40s on the Path to Freedom offers a comprehensive guide to the art of persuasion and influence. By applying these techniques, over 40 men and women can transform their mindset, break free from limitations, and achieve the freedom they desire. Embrace the power of persuasion and influence, and unlock your true potential on the path to freedom.

Chapter 6: Setting and Achieving Goals for Lasting Transformation

The Importance of Goal Setting in Unlocking True Potential

In the journey of life, we often find ourselves at crossroads, questioning our purpose and seeking a sense of freedom. As men and women over 40, we have accumulated a wealth of experiences, successes, and challenges. However, we may also feel trapped in the monotony of our daily routines, yearning for something more fulfilling. It is during these moments that goal setting becomes crucial in unlocking our true potential and attaining the freedom we desire.

Goal setting is a powerful tool that allows us to establish a clear direction and purpose in our lives. By defining our goals, we create a roadmap that guides us towards the life we envision. Through the lens of Neuro-Linguistic Programming

(NLP) techniques, goal setting takes on a whole new level of efficacy, empowering our mindset and transforming our lives.

NLP for mindset transformation is a niche that offers incredible opportunities for personal growth and self-discovery. By incorporating NLP techniques into our goal-setting process, we can tap into our subconscious mind, reprogram limiting beliefs, and unleash our hidden potential. This opens up a world of possibilities, enabling us to break free from self-imposed limitations and embrace a life of freedom.

When we set goals, we ignite a fire within us, fueling our motivation and perseverance. It gives us a sense of purpose and direction, allowing us to focus our energy on what truly matters. Without clear goals, we risk drifting through life without a sense of fulfillment or accomplishment. However, by setting specific, measurable, achievable, relevant, and time-bound (SMART) goals, we take ownership of our lives and unlock our true potential.

Goal setting also brings clarity to our actions, ensuring that we make conscious choices aligned with our aspirations. It helps us overcome obstacles and navigate through adversity by reminding us of our ultimate destination. As we progress towards our goals, we gain confidence, resilience, and a deep sense of fulfillment. Our self-belief strengthens, and we realize that true freedom lies not in external circumstances but in our ability to shape our own destiny.

In conclusion, the importance of goal setting in unlocking true potential cannot be overstated. As men and women over 40 seeking freedom, incorporating NLP techniques into our goal-setting process empowers us to transform our mindset and unlock our hidden potential. It grants us the clarity, motivation, and direction needed to break free from limitations and live a life of true fulfillment. Embrace the power of goal setting, and witness the incredible transformation that unfolds on your path to freedom.

Creating SMART Goals for Over 40s on the Path to Freedom

In our journey towards personal growth and achieving true freedom, setting clear and achievable goals is essential. As we navigate the challenges and opportunities that come with being over 40, it becomes even more crucial to adopt a strategic approach to goal-setting. This subchapter will guide you through the process of creating SMART goals using NLP techniques, empowering you to unlock your true potential.

SMART goals are specific, measurable, attainable, relevant, and time-bound. By incorporating these elements into your goal-setting process, you will be able to create a roadmap that maximizes your chances of success. Let's delve into each component in detail:

1. Specific: Define your goals with precision. Instead of saying "I want more freedom," be specific about what freedom means to you. For example, "I want to have the financial freedom to retire comfortably by 55."

2. Measurable: Establish criteria to quantify your progress. This enables you to track your achievements and stay motivated. For instance, "I will save $500 per month towards my retirement fund."

3. Attainable: Set goals that are within your reach. Consider your current circumstances, resources, and abilities. Setting realistic goals will prevent discouragement and increase your chances of success. For example, "I will increase my income by 10% within the next year by seeking a promotion or exploring new opportunities."

4. Relevant: Align your goals with your long-term vision and values. Ensure they contribute to your overall sense of freedom and fulfillment. For instance, "I will prioritize self-care by dedicating 30 minutes every day to meditation or exercise."

5. Time-bound: Set deadlines to create a sense of urgency and accountability. This helps you stay focused and motivated. For example, "I will complete a certification course in my field within the next six months to expand my career options."

By implementing these SMART goal-setting techniques, you will be better equipped to transform your mindset and achieve the freedom you desire. Through the power of NLP, you can reprogram your beliefs, overcome limiting patterns, and harness your full potential. Remember, the journey to freedom is unique for each individual, but by setting SMART goals, you are laying a solid foundation for success.

Whether you are seeking financial freedom, personal fulfillment, or a healthier lifestyle, NLP techniques combined with SMART goals can guide you towards your desired outcomes. Embrace the power of goal-setting and unlock your true potential today!

Overcoming Procrastination and Building Consistency

In today's fast-paced world, it's easy to fall into the trap of procrastination. For many individuals over the age of 40, this can become a major obstacle on the path to freedom. Whether you're looking to achieve personal goals, career success, or simply experience a greater sense of fulfillment, overcoming procrastination and building consistency is essential. In this subchapter, we will explore the powerful techniques of Neuro-Linguistic Programming (NLP) that can help transform your mindset, enabling you to overcome procrastination and build the consistency needed to unlock your true potential.

Procrastination is often rooted in negative thought patterns and limiting beliefs that hold us back from taking action. As we age, these patterns can become deeply ingrained, making it even more challenging to break free. However, with the right tools and strategies, it is possible to reprogram your mind and develop new habits that foster consistency and productivity.

NLP offers a range of techniques that can help shift your mindset and overcome procrastination. By understanding the language of your mind and the impact it has on your behavior, you can begin to reframe negative thoughts and replace them with positive affirmations. Through visualization exercises and mental rehearsal, you can create a clear vision of your goals, making them feel more attainable and compelling.

Additionally, NLP techniques such as anchoring and pattern interruption can be powerful tools in combating procrastination. By associating a specific physical or mental state with a desired behavior, you can create triggers that automatically propel you into action. Furthermore, learning to interrupt negative patterns of thought and replace them with empowering ones can help break the cycle of procrastination.

Building consistency is equally important on the journey to freedom. NLP techniques can assist in developing effective habits and routines that support your goals. By creating a detailed plan and breaking it down into manageable steps, you can build momentum and make consistent progress. NLP also emphasizes the power of modeling successful individuals, allowing you to learn from their habits and apply them to your own life.

In conclusion, overcoming procrastination and building consistency is crucial for individuals over 40 seeking freedom and personal growth. NLP techniques provide a powerful framework for transforming your mindset and developing habits that support your goals. By implementing these strategies, you can unlock your true potential and experience a greater sense of fulfillment in all areas of life.

Chapter 7: Cultivating a Positive Mindset for Sustainable Change

Developing Resilience in the Face of Challenges

In life, we all face challenges that can sometimes feel overwhelming. Whether it's a career setback, a personal loss, or a health issue, these obstacles can test our strength and resilience. However, it is during these difficult times that our true potential is revealed. In this subchapter, we will explore the concept of developing resilience and how NLP techniques can help individuals over the age of 40 unlock their true potential and find freedom.

Resilience is the ability to bounce back from adversity, to adapt and grow despite facing challenges. For those in their 40s and beyond, life can present unique obstacles, such as career transitions, empty nest syndrome, or feelings of stagnation. By applying NLP techniques, individuals can transform their mindset and develop the resilience needed to navigate these challenges with grace and confidence.

One powerful NLP technique for building resilience is reframing. Reframing involves shifting our perspective on a situation or challenge. Instead of viewing setbacks as failures, we can reframe them as opportunities for growth and learning. By reframing our experiences, we can cultivate a positive mindset and develop the resilience to overcome obstacles.

Another NLP technique that can be particularly effective for those over 40 is anchoring. Anchoring involves creating a physical or mental cue that triggers a positive emotional state. By anchoring ourselves to feelings of strength, courage, and resilience, we can access these inner resources whenever we face challenges. Anchoring can help individuals stay grounded and focused, even in the face of adversity.

In addition to these techniques, self-reflection and self-compassion are essential for developing resilience. Taking the time to understand our strengths, values, and goals can provide a solid foundation for navigating challenges. By practicing self- compassion, we can acknowledge our efforts and progress, even when things don't go as planned.

Ultimately, developing resilience is a lifelong journey. As we age, it becomes even more crucial to cultivate the inner strength to face challenges head-on. By incorporating NLP techniques into our mindset transformation, individuals over 40 can unlock their true potential and find the freedom to embrace life's challenges with resilience, confidence, and grace.

In "Unlocking Your True Potential: NLP Techniques for Over 40s on the Path to Freedom," readers will find practical exercises, real-life stories, and step-by-step guidance to help them develop resilience and overcome the challenges they may encounter on their journey towards personal freedom. Through NLP, individuals can tap into their inner power and transform their mindset, allowing them to navigate life's ups and downs with resilience and unwavering determination.

Practicing Gratitude and Appreciation for Freedom and Happiness

In our journey towards achieving true freedom and happiness, it is essential to understand the power of practicing gratitude and appreciation. As we navigate through life, especially in our 40s and beyond, we may encounter various challenges and obstacles that can hinder our sense of freedom. However, by incorporating NLP techniques into our mindset transformation, we can cultivate a deep sense of gratitude and appreciation, ultimately unlocking our true potential.

Gratitude is the practice of acknowledging and being thankful for the blessings and positive aspects of our lives. It is about shifting our focus from what is lacking to what we already have. By adopting an attitude of gratitude, we can begin to appreciate the freedom we currently possess, whether it be our health, relationships, or career opportunities. Gratitude allows us to recognize the abundance in our lives and fosters a mindset of positivity and contentment.

NLP techniques can help us reframe our thoughts and beliefs, enabling us to see the world through a lens of gratitude. By identifying and challenging negative thought patterns, we can replace them with empowering ones that promote gratitude and appreciation. This transformation of mindset not only brings us closer to freedom but also enhances our overall well-being and happiness.

Appreciation goes hand in hand with gratitude. While gratitude focuses on the present, appreciation encourages us to reflect on the past and recognize the experiences and lessons that have shaped us. By acknowledging the challenges we have overcome and the growth we have achieved, we can foster a deep sense of appreciation for our journey. This newfound appreciation empowers us to embrace our freedom and live life to the fullest, knowing that every experience has contributed to our personal growth.

Practicing gratitude and appreciation is not just a one-time exercise but a daily habit that we need to cultivate. By incorporating simple practices such as keeping a gratitude journal, expressing thanks to others, or engaging in mindfulness exercises, we can strengthen our ability to find joy and freedom in every aspect of our lives.

In conclusion, for men and women over 40 seeking freedom, incorporating the power of gratitude and appreciation through NLP techniques can be transformative. By shifting our mindset and focusing on the blessings and growth in our lives, we can unlock our true potential and live a life of freedom and happiness. Embracing gratitude and appreciation will not only enhance our well-being but also inspire and empower others to do the same. Let us embark on this journey together, and unlock the door to our true potential.

Fostering a Growth Mindset for Continuous Personal Growth

In our journey towards personal growth and finding true freedom, one of the most powerful tools at our disposal is the concept of a growth mindset. This subchapter will delve into how fostering a growth mindset using Neuro-Linguistic Programming (NLP) techniques can transform our mindset and propel us towards unlimited personal growth, especially for individuals over 40.

As we age, it's common to feel stuck in our ways or believe that personal growth becomes more challenging. However, with the right mindset and the application of NLP techniques, we can overcome these limitations and unlock our true potential.

A growth mindset is the belief that our abilities and intelligence can be developed through dedication, effort, and a willingness to embrace challenges. It is the understanding that our talents and skills are not fixed traits, but rather qualities that can be nurtured and expanded upon. By adopting a growth mindset, we can break free from self-imposed limitations and open ourselves to continuous personal growth.

NLP techniques offer practical strategies for cultivating a growth mindset. One such technique is reframing, which involves shifting our perspective to see challenges as opportunities for growth. Instead of viewing failure as a setback, we can reframe it as a valuable learning experience that propels us forward. Through NLP, we can rewire our thought patterns and replace self-limiting beliefs with empowering ones.

Another powerful NLP technique is visualization. By vividly imagining ourselves achieving our goals and living our desired life, we create a compelling vision that fuels our motivation and helps us stay focused on our path to freedom. Through visualization, we tap into the power of our subconscious mind to manifest the reality we desire.

Furthermore, NLP offers techniques for improving self-awareness and enhancing communication skills, which are crucial for personal growth. By understanding our thought processes, emotions, and behaviors, we can identify and overcome any self-sabotaging patterns that hinder our progress. Additionally, NLP techniques can help us build rapport with others, enabling us to create meaningful connections and leverage support networks in our journey towards freedom.

In conclusion, fostering a growth mindset through NLP techniques is a powerful tool for continuous personal growth, especially for individuals over 40 seeking freedom. By reframing challenges, visualizing success, improving self-awareness, and enhancing communication skills, we can break free from self-imposed limitations and unlock our true potential. With a growth mindset, we can embrace change, overcome obstacles, and achieve the freedom we desire.

Chapter 8: Unlocking Your True Potential for Freedom and Fulfillment

Embracing Change and Stepping Out of Your Comfort Zone

In our journey towards personal growth and self-discovery, change is inevitable. As we age, it becomes even more crucial to embrace change and step out of our comfort zones to unlock our true potential and attain the freedom we desire. This chapter will explore the power of Neuro-Linguistic Programming (NLP) techniques to help men and women over 40 navigate this transformational path.

One of the fundamental principles of NLP is that our mindset plays a crucial role in shaping our reality. Many of us have developed patterns of thinking and behavior that have kept us confined within the boundaries of our comfort zones. While comfort zones provide a sense of security, they also limit our growth and hinder us from experiencing the true freedom we desire.

To break free from these limitations, we must first recognize the power of change. Change is not something to be feared but rather embraced as an opportunity for growth. By shifting our mindset and adopting a growth mindset, we can view change as a stepping stone towards personal evolution.

Stepping out of our comfort zones requires courage and a willingness to face the unknown. NLP techniques can be incredibly effective in helping us overcome the fear and resistance associated with change. Through techniques such as reframing, visualization, and anchoring, we can reprogram our minds to embrace change as an exciting adventure rather than a daunting challenge.

Moreover, NLP provides us with tools to identify and replace limiting beliefs that hold us back from stepping out of our comfort zones. By reframing our thoughts and beliefs, we can create empowering narratives that propel us towards our desired freedom.

This chapter will also delve into practical exercises and strategies to support your journey of embracing change. From setting achievable goals and taking small steps towards change to cultivating a supportive network and practicing self-care, we will explore various techniques to facilitate your transformation.

Remember, age should never be a barrier to personal growth and freedom. By harnessing the power of NLP and embracing change, you can unlock your true potential and embark on a fulfilling journey towards the freedom you deserve. It's time to step out of your comfort zone and experience the joy and liberation that await you on the other side.

Finding Purpose and Passion in Life after 40

As we reach our 40s, it is natural to start questioning the purpose and passion in our lives. We may begin to feel a sense of restlessness or dissatisfaction, wondering if there is more to life than what we have experienced thus far. This chapter is dedicated to helping over 40 men and women find their true purpose and unlock their passion, using Neuro-Linguistic Programming (NLP) techniques for mindset transformation.

NLP is a powerful tool that can assist in reshaping our thoughts, beliefs, and behaviors. It allows us to tap into our subconscious mind and unlock our true potential. Through NLP, we can identify the limiting beliefs that have been holding us back and replace them with empowering ones. This process is crucial in finding our purpose and passion, as it helps us align our thoughts and actions with our deepest desires.

The first step in this journey is self-reflection. Take the time to examine your life and identify what truly brings you joy and fulfillment. What are your core values, and how can you incorporate them into your daily routine? By understanding ourselves on a deeper level, we can begin to shape our lives in a way that aligns with our true purpose.

Next, it is essential to let go of any fears or doubts that may be holding us back. Often, as we get older, we become more risk-averse, fearing failure or judgment. However, true freedom lies in embracing our passions and pursuing them wholeheartedly. NLP techniques can help us reframe our fears and transform them into motivation and courage.

Another powerful NLP tool for mindset transformation is visualization. By creating a vivid mental image of ourselves living our purpose and pursuing our passions, we can manifest these desires into reality. Visualization allows us to tap into the power of our subconscious mind and attract the opportunities and experiences that will guide us towards our true path.

Finally, it is crucial to surround ourselves with a supportive community. Connecting with like-minded individuals who are also on a quest for purpose and passion can provide valuable insights and encouragement. Whether it be joining a meetup group, attending workshops, or seeking out a mentor, finding a community that supports our growth can make all the difference.

In conclusion, finding purpose and passion in life after 40 is a journey that requires self-reflection, letting go of fears, visualization, and building a supportive community. By utilizing NLP techniques for mindset transformation, we can unlock our true potential and create a life of freedom and fulfillment. It is never too late to discover our purpose and live a life filled with passion. The path is right in front of us

- all we need to do is take the first step.

Celebrating Success and Sustaining Your Transformation

Subchapter: Celebrating Success and Sustaining Your Transformation Introduction:

Congratulations on your journey towards unlocking your true potential! As you continue to explore the powerful techniques of Neuro-Linguistic Programming (NLP) for mindset transformation, it is essential to celebrate your successes and find ways to sustain the positive changes you have experienced. This subchapter will guide you on how to celebrate your accomplishments and provide valuable strategies to maintain your newfound freedom.

1. The Importance of Celebrating Success:
In the pursuit of personal growth and transformation, it is crucial to acknowledge and celebrate your achievements along the way. Celebrating success not only boosts your motivation but also reinforces the positive changes you have made. It acts as a reminder of your progress and encourages you to continue your journey towards freedom.

2. Reflecting on Your Transformation:

Take a moment to reflect on the changes you have experienced since embarking on this path. Consider the mindset shifts, limiting beliefs you have overcome, and the new empowering habits you have adopted. Journaling about your transformational journey can be an excellent way to gain clarity and appreciation for your progress.

3. Celebratory Rituals:

Create rituals to mark and celebrate your successes. These rituals can be as simple as treating yourself to a special meal, indulging in a relaxing spa day, or taking a well-deserved vacation. By intentionally setting aside time to acknowledge your accomplishments, you reinforce the positive neural connections formed during your transformation process.

4. Gratitude Practice:

An essential aspect of sustaining your transformation is cultivating gratitude. Take a few moments each day to focus on the things you are grateful for in your life. This practice helps shift your mindset towards positivity and abundance, further enhancing your freedom and overall well-being.

5. Building a Supportive Community:

Surround yourself with like-minded individuals who support your journey towards freedom. Connect with others who are also interested in mindset transformation and NLP techniques. Joining support groups, attending workshops, or finding an accountability partner can provide the necessary encouragement and inspiration to continue growing and sustaining your transformation.

Conclusion:

As you celebrate your successes and sustain your transformation, remember that your journey towards freedom is an ongoing process. Embrace the power of NLP techniques and mindset transformation, and continue to unlock your true potential. By celebrating your accomplishments and implementing strategies to maintain your progress, you can experience lasting change and enjoy the freedom you desire. Keep pushing forward, and the possibilities for personal growth and transformation are endless.

Chapter 9: NLP Techniques for Overcoming Obstacles and Creating Freedom

Overcoming Fear and Building Courage for Personal Growth

Fear is a powerful emotion that can hold us back from reaching our true potential. It is a natural response to perceived threats or dangers, but oftentimes, it becomes an obstacle that prevents us from experiencing personal growth and attaining the freedom we desire. In this subchapter, we will explore effective techniques from Neuro-Linguistic Programming (NLP) that can help you overcome fear and build the courage needed for personal growth.

As men and women over 40, we have accumulated a lifetime of experiences that have shaped our beliefs and mindset.

It is common to develop fears and limiting beliefs as a result of past traumas or negative experiences. However, it is important to recognize that fear is merely a perception, and with the right tools, we can reframe our mindset and overcome it.

NLP offers powerful techniques for mindset transformation, enabling us to break free from fear and unlock our true potential. One such technique is called "reframing," which involves altering the way we perceive a situation or fear. By reframing our thoughts, we can change our emotional response and develop a more empowering perspective.

Another effective NLP technique is "anchoring." This technique involves associating a specific state of mind or emotion with a physical touch or gesture. By creating an anchor, we can access courage and confidence whenever we need it. For example, if public speaking is a fear, we can create an anchor by touching our thumb and index finger together while feeling confident and courageous. Then, whenever we face a public speaking opportunity, we can activate the anchor to tap into that empowering state of mind.

Additionally, NLP offers techniques for desensitizing fears through gradual exposure and visualization. By gradually exposing ourselves to our fears in a safe and controlled manner, we can diminish their power over us. Visualization exercises can also help reprogram our subconscious mind, enabling us to visualize ourselves overcoming our fears and achieving our goals.

Building courage for personal growth is a journey that requires commitment and practice. By incorporating these NLP techniques into our daily lives, we can overcome fear and experience the freedom we desire. Remember that fear is just an illusion, and with the right mindset, we can conquer it and unlock our true potential.

If you are an over 40 man or woman seeking freedom and personal growth, NLP techniques for mindset transformation offer a powerful toolkit to help you overcome your fears. Embrace the power of reframing, anchoring, desensitization, and visualization to unlock your true potential and live a life free from the limitations of fear. Start your journey today and discover the courage within you to embrace personal growth and the freedom it brings.

NLP Techniques for Breaking Free from Limiting Patterns and Habits

In our journey towards personal growth and self-discovery, we often find ourselves trapped in limiting patterns and habits that prevent us from reaching our true potential. These patterns may be deeply ingrained in our subconscious mind, making it challenging to break free from their grip. However, with the power of Neuro-Linguistic Programming (NLP), we can unlock the doors to our true freedom.

NLP is a powerful tool for mindset transformation, specifically designed to help individuals overcome their limiting beliefs and patterns. It focuses on the connection between our thoughts, language, and behavior, allowing us to reprogram our minds for success and personal fulfillment. As men and women over 40, we have accumulated years of experiences and conditioning that may have shaped our thoughts and limited our possibilities. NLP offers us a way to break free from these constraints and create a life of freedom and abundance.

One of the fundamental techniques in NLP for breaking free from limiting patterns and habits is called reframing. Reframing allows us to shift our perception of a situation, enabling us to see it from a different perspective. By reframing our thoughts, we can challenge the beliefs that hold us back and create new empowering meanings. This technique is particularly effective for transforming negative self-talk and self-doubt into positive affirmations and confidence.

Another powerful NLP technique is called anchoring. Anchoring enables us to associate a specific emotion or state of mind with a physical or mental trigger. By creating an anchor, we can access empowering states whenever we need them. For example, if we tend to feel anxious or overwhelmed in certain situations, we can anchor a state of calmness and confidence to a specific gesture or word.

Whenever we encounter those situations again, we can activate the anchor and instantly change our emotional state.

Additionally, NLP offers techniques such as timeline therapy and parts integration, which allow us to release negative emotions from past experiences and integrate conflicting parts of ourselves. These techniques help us let go of emotional baggage that may be holding us back and enable us to align our thoughts, beliefs, and actions towards our true desires.

By applying these NLP techniques, we can break free from limiting patterns and habits, reprogram our minds for success, and unlock our true potential. As men and women over 40 looking for freedom, NLP offers us a transformative path towards personal growth, self-discovery, and a life of fulfillment. Embrace the power of NLP and embark on a journey to unlock your true potential. The freedom you seek is within reach.

Harnessing the Power of Neuro-Linguistic Programming for Freedom

In today's fast-paced and demanding world, finding true freedom can often feel like an elusive goal. As individuals in their 40s and beyond, many of us have spent years feeling trapped by societal expectations, limiting beliefs, and negative thought patterns. However, there is a powerful tool that can help us break free from these constraints and unlock our true potential: Neuro-Linguistic Programming (NLP).

NLP is a transformative approach to personal development that focuses on the connection between our thoughts, language, and behavior. By understanding how our minds work and learning to reprogram our thought patterns, we can create lasting change in our lives and experience true freedom.

One of the key areas where NLP can be incredibly effective is in mindset transformation. As we age, we often find ourselves caught up in negative thinking patterns that hold us back from living the life we truly desire. We may believe that it's too late to pursue our dreams or that we're not capable of achieving success. NLP techniques can help us challenge and reframe these limiting beliefs, allowing us to cultivate a mindset of abundance, possibility, and freedom.

Through NLP, we can learn to harness the power of our minds to create the life we truly desire. By using techniques such as visualization, affirmations, and anchoring, we can reprogram our subconscious minds to align with our goals and aspirations. We can let go of self-doubt and fear, and instead, cultivate confidence, resilience, and a sense of empowerment.

Furthermore, NLP can also help us improve our communication skills, both with ourselves and with others. By understanding the language patterns we use and how they impact our thoughts and emotions, we can enhance our ability to express ourselves effectively and build stronger relationships. This newfound communication mastery can open doors to new opportunities, deepen connections, and foster a sense of freedom in our interactions with others.

In "Unlocking Your True Potential: NLP Techniques for Over 40s on the Path to Freedom," we delve deep into the world of NLP and provide a comprehensive guide to harnessing its power for mindset transformation. Through practical exercises, real-life examples, and step-by-step instructions, this book empowers men and women over 40 to break free from limiting beliefs, overcome obstacles, and create a life of freedom and fulfillment.

If you're seeking true freedom in your life, it's time to unlock your true potential through the power of Neuro-Linguistic Programming. Embrace the transformative techniques outlined in this book, and embark on a journey of self-discovery, growth, and liberation. The path to freedom awaits, and NLP is the key to unlock its doors.

Chapter 10: Embracing Freedom and Living a Life of Fulfillment

Maintaining Balance and Wellbeing in All Areas of Life

In today's fast-paced and demanding world, it can be easy to lose sight of our personal wellbeing and the need for balance in all areas of our lives. As men and women over 40 who are seeking freedom and empowerment, it is crucial to prioritize our mental, emotional, and physical health. This subchapter will delve into the powerful NLP techniques that can help you achieve and maintain equilibrium in your life, allowing you to unlock your true potential.

One of the fundamental principles of NLP for mindset transformation is the recognition that our thoughts and beliefs shape our reality. By harnessing the power of your mind, you can cultivate a positive and balanced mindset that will permeate all aspects of your life. Through various NLP techniques such as reframing and anchoring, you will learn how to rewire your thought patterns and overcome limiting beliefs that may be holding you back from achieving true freedom.

Achieving balance and wellbeing requires a holistic approach that encompasses different areas of life. This subchapter will explore how you can strike a harmonious equilibrium between your personal and professional life, relationships, physical health, and self-care. By setting clear boundaries and priorities, you can ensure that your time and energy are allocated in a way that nurtures your wellbeing and supports your goals.

Furthermore, this subchapter will delve into the importance of self-care and stress management. As individuals in the prime of their lives, it is crucial for you to prioritize self-care practices that nourish your mind, body, and soul. Whether it's practicing mindfulness, engaging in regular physical activity, or carving out time for hobbies and passions, these small acts of self-care can have a profound impact on your overall wellbeing and sense of freedom.

Lastly, this subchapter will provide practical strategies for maintaining balance and wellbeing in the face of challenges and setbacks. Life is full of ups and downs, and it is essential to have tools and techniques at your disposal to navigate through these turbulent times. By embracing resilience, cultivating a growth mindset, and utilizing NLP techniques such as timeline therapy, you will develop the inner strength and resources necessary to overcome obstacles and thrive in all areas of your life.

In conclusion, maintaining balance and wellbeing is a lifelong journey that requires conscious effort and dedication. As men and women over 40 seeking freedom, the NLP techniques explored in this subchapter will empower you to unlock your true potential and live a life that is rich in happiness, fulfillment, and overall wellbeing. By incorporating these practices into your daily life, you will not only transform your mindset but also experience a newfound sense of freedom in all areas of your life.

Nurturing Relationships and Creating Supportive Networks

In the journey towards unlocking your true potential and attaining freedom, one aspect that cannot be overlooked is the power of nurturing relationships and creating supportive networks. As individuals over the age of 40, we have accumulated experiences, wisdom, and insights that can greatly benefit our personal and professional growth. However, it is essential to harness the power of our connections to maximize our transformational journey using Neuro-Linguistic Programming (NLP) techniques.

NLP for mindset transformation offers us a powerful toolset to rewire our thoughts, beliefs, and behaviors. However, we must recognize that human beings are social creatures who thrive in the presence of genuine connections. By nurturing relationships, we create an environment that fosters growth, encouragement, and support.

Firstly, it is crucial to cultivate strong connections with like-minded individuals who are also seeking personal growth and freedom. Surrounding ourselves with individuals who share similar goals and values allows us to exchange ideas, provide motivation, and hold each other accountable. These supportive networks act as a catalyst for transformation by fostering a sense of belonging and providing a space for open and honest dialogue.

Furthermore, nurturing relationships within our existing social circles, such as family and friends, is equally important. These connections provide a sense of stability, love, and understanding. By sharing our aspirations, challenges, and victories with our loved ones, we strengthen our bonds and gain valuable insights from their perspectives. Their support and encouragement can fuel our motivation to overcome obstacles and continue on our path towards freedom.

Additionally, NLP techniques can be utilized to enhance our communication skills, enabling us to build deeper and more meaningful connections. By mastering the art of rapport-building, active listening, and effective communication, we can create an environment of trust, empathy, and understanding. Such skills not only strengthen our existing relationships but also open doors to new connections and opportunities.

In conclusion, as individuals over 40 seeking freedom and personal growth, nurturing relationships and creating supportive networks is a vital component of our journey. By surrounding ourselves with like-minded individuals, cultivating connections within our existing social circles, and honing our communication skills using NLP techniques, we can create an environment that fosters growth, motivation, and empowerment. Remember, true freedom is not achieved in isolation but through the power of human connections. Embrace the transformative potential of nurturing relationships and watch as they unlock your true potential on the path to freedom.

Embracing Freedom as a Lifelong Journey

In our book, "Unlocking Your True Potential: NLP Techniques for Over 40s on the Path to Freedom," we address the specific needs and desires of men and women over 40 who are seeking a sense of freedom in their lives. For this audience, freedom is not just a fleeting moment or a one-time achievement, but rather a lifelong journey towards self-actualization and personal transformation. And at the core of this journey lies the power of Neuro-Linguistic Programming (NLP) techniques for mindset transformation.

As we enter our 40s and beyond, many of us find ourselves reflecting on the choices we've made, the dreams we've left behind, and the limitations we've imposed upon ourselves. It is at this stage that we start to yearn for freedom – freedom from self-doubt, limiting beliefs, and societal expectations.

We understand that true freedom is not about escaping responsibilities or obligations, but rather about embracing our authentic selves and living a life aligned with our deepest desires.

NLP offers a powerful toolkit for breaking free from the shackles of our past conditioning and creating a mindset that empowers us to live our best lives. Through various techniques such as reframing, anchoring, and modeling, we can rewire our neural pathways and transform our thoughts, emotions, and behaviors. NLP helps us uncover and challenge the limiting beliefs that have held us back, replacing them with new empowering beliefs that propel us forward on our path to freedom.

Embracing freedom as a lifelong journey requires self-awareness, courage, and a willingness to let go of what no longer serves us. It is about recognizing that we have the power to choose our own thoughts, interpret our experiences, and shape our reality. NLP enables us to develop a growth mindset, cultivate resilience, and embrace change as an opportunity for growth rather than a threat.

In this subchapter, we delve into the intricacies of embracing freedom as a lifelong journey, providing practical exercises, case studies, and real-life examples that illustrate the transformative power of NLP techniques. We explore how to navigate the challenges and roadblocks that may arise along the way, offering guidance on how to maintain motivation, overcome setbacks, and stay committed to our path of personal liberation.

For over 40 men and women looking for freedom, this subchapter serves as a guidebook, offering insights, strategies, and inspiration to unlock their true potential. It is an invitation to embark on an empowering journey of self-discovery, growth, and transformation – a journey that leads to a life of authenticity, fulfillment, and freedom.

Conclusion: Embrace Your True Potential and Live a Life of Freedom and Fulfillment

Congratulations! You have taken the first step towards unlocking your true potential and embarking on a journey towards a life of freedom and fulfillment. Throughout this book, we have explored the powerful techniques of Neuro-Linguistic Programming (NLP) to transform your mindset and empower you to live your best life. Now, it is time to bring it all together and embrace the amazing possibilities that await you.

As men and women over 40, we often find ourselves in a pivotal moment of self- reflection. We may have achieved success in our careers or raised a family, but deep down, we know there is more to life than what we have experienced so far. We yearn for a sense of freedom and fulfillment that goes beyond societal expectations and limitations.

NLP offers us the tools to break free from the constraints of our past and create a future filled with purpose and joy. By understanding the power of our thoughts, language, and behavior, we can reprogram our minds to align with our true desires and aspirations. No longer will we be held back by limiting beliefs or negative patterns that have hindered our progress in the past.

Through the techniques learned in this book, you have discovered how to reframe your mindset, overcome obstacles, and tap into your inner resources. You have learned to cultivate empowering beliefs, set compelling goals, and create a roadmap for success. But more importantly, you have learned to embrace your true potential.

Living a life of freedom and fulfillment means daring to dream big and taking courageous action to bring those dreams to life. It means shedding the expectations and limitations that society or others have placed upon us. It means embracing our uniqueness and pursuing our passions with unwavering determination.

Remember, true freedom comes from within. It is not about external circumstances or material possessions. It is about living in alignment with our values, following our intuition, and making choices that are true to who we are. It is about embracing every moment and finding joy in the journey.

So, my dear friends, as you close this chapter and embark on your personal journey towards freedom, know that you have the power within you to create a life of unlimited possibilities. Embrace your true potential, for it is only through embracing who we truly are that we can live a life of freedom and fulfillment. The path may not always be easy, but with NLP as your guide, you have the tools to overcome any obstacles that come your way.

Now go forth, embrace your true potential, and live a life of freedom and fulfillment that you truly deserve!